The Wild West in American History

TRAPPERS & TRADERS

Written by Gail Stewart
Illustrated by Tom Casmer/Spectrum Studios
Edited by Mark E. Ahlstrom

LIBRARY OF CONGRESS
Library of Congress Cataloging-in-Publication Data

Stewart, Gail, 1949-
    Trappers and traders / Gail B. Stewart.
      p. cm. -- (The Wild West in American history)
    Summary: Describes the life and activities of the trappers and fur traders
in the Old West in the first half of the nineteenth century and recounts
stories of such colorful individuals as Jim Bridger and John Colter.
    ISBN 0-86625-401-3
    1. West (U.S.)--History--To 1848--Juvenile literature. 2. West (U.S.)--
Description and travel--To 1848--Juvenile literature. 3. Trappers--West (U.S.)
--History--Juvenile literature. 4. Fur traders--West (U.S.)--History--Juvenile
literature. [1. Trappers--West (U.S.) 2. Fur traders--West (U.S.) 3. Frontier
and pioneer life--West (U.S.) 4. West (U.S.)--History--To 1848.] I. Title.
II. Series.
                                                              89-35574
          978   CIP
                                                              AC

Rourke Publications, Inc.
Vero Beach, Florida, 32964

TRAPPERS & TRADERS

TRAPPERS & TRADERS

Trappers and traders are cloaked in legend. Their exploits—encounters with hostile Indians, grizzly bears, and other hazards—are the things of which campfire legends are made. Yet historians say that the role played by the trappers and traders of the Old West was not legend at all. It was real.

There were probably 300 of them—350 at most. They endured the worst living conditions imaginable. Living more than 1,000 miles from any town or settlement, they ate nothing but meat (about eight pounds of it per day) and drank nothing but water. They had shoulder-length hair and wore greasy, stiff animal skins. In the years that they roamed the mountains and forests, more than half were killed by Indians. Others were so respected by Native Americans that they were made tribal chiefs!

They were the first white men who learned the way through the Rocky Mountains, and the first people to figure out the routes from St. Louis to the California coast. They established lines of communication with many of the Indian tribes, and because of this they learned a great deal of valuable information about surviving in the wilderness. Much of this information was passed on to others years later. More than a few of these men became scouts for wagon trains and the U.S. Army after their trapping and trading days were over.

Many trappers and traders were educated—a few could speak several languages. Still others, perhaps the vast majority, were uneducated men.

Looking down on men who were satisfied with cities, towns, and farms, the trappers and traders of the Old West endured the misery of their lives because they were sure that their freedom was well worth it. Responsible for no one and to no one, they needed agility, bravery, and quick wits to survive.

A NEW TERRITORY

*I*n the early years of the 19th century, America was full of promise. It was a free country, having recently won its independence from England. It was a land whose people had every reason to believe that prosperity and good fortune were theirs for the taking.

One of the things that made early Americans so optimistic was the vast, uncharted land that lay to the west. Back in 1800, "west" meant Illinois, or Missouri. No one really knew what lay beyond the Mississippi River, or even how far the land stretched. It was simply exciting to know that the land was there. There was a sense that Americans could stretch beyond their early boundaries.

It was in 1803 that Napoleon Bonaparte, the French emperor, sold to the United States a huge chunk of land. This Louisiana Territory, as it was called, ranged from Canada to the Gulf of Mexico, and from the Mississippi River to the Rocky Mountains.

After the deal was signed, U.S. President Thomas Jefferson was eager to find out just what sort of land he had purchased. Was it, as some suggested, a vast desert inhabited by fierce Indian tribes? Or was there farmland, or plains, or forest?

Jefferson persuaded Congress to spend $2,500 of the nation's money on finding out the answer to these questions. He hired his personal secretary, Merriwether Lewis, and Lewis' good friend, William Clark, to lead an expedition. The two men, along with 45 hand-picked men from the army, would explore the Louisiana

Merriwether Lewis
(Photo: Oregon Historical Society.)

William Clark
(Photo: Oregon Historical Society.)

Territory and bring back detailed journals of what they found. The Lewis and Clark Expedition left St. Louis in 1804. When they returned two years later, they brought back tales of a wonderful land. They had gone beyond the western boundary of the Louisiana Territory, traveling all the way to the Pacific Ocean. In all, the land stretched for 2,000 miles. There were shimmering lakes and crystal-clear rivers brimming with fish. There were forests filled with game, and more fox, deer, and beaver than the men had ever seen before! Finally, there were Indians, thousands and thousands of them. The explorers reported that they'd had no trouble getting along with the Indians they had encountered.

The eyewitness accounts of what lay beyond the Mississippi River seem to have set off a rush of men not wanting to be left out of a good thing. Some were trappers, who were lured by the thought of getting rich by trapping animals and selling pelts, or animal furs. Some were traders, eager to get rich by trading with trappers and Indians who possessed these valuable pelts. So it was that both traders and trappers began opening the West, preceding all the settlers and wagon trains filled with pioneers looking for homes.

Lewis and Clark returned with tales about the rich and beautiful land they had seen.

THE MOST PRIZED FUR IN THE WORLD

*I*t wasn't a big variety of pelts that these trappers and traders were after. In fact, it wasn't even an assortment of two or three.

One animal was prized for its wonderfully thick, soft fur. You might think it would be a large animal like a mountain lion, or a ferocious animal, like a timberwolf. If so, you would be wrong. The object of all the trapping in the Old West was a large brownish-black rodent with a flat tail—the beaver.

Beaver pelts were the most sought-after fur in the world for hundreds of years. The chief use for the pelts was in the making of beaver-felt hats. More than 100,000 beaver pelts were sold every year to hatmakers in many different countries.

The long hair on the surface of the pelt was trimmed off. It wasn't important—rather, it was the downy-soft underfur that the hatmakers

prized. It had a thick, velvet texture that was like no other fur in the world. The underfur was flattened, covered with wet cloth, and treated with special acids to make it durable. Then it was beaten to make it more pliable so it could be shaped in any number of styles. Some people liked the tall stovepipe hats. Others preferred the bicorn, the tricorn, or the low-slung Quaker hat. Styles came and went, but the material for each new type of hat was beaver fur.

It's odd to think of fashion being such an important force in the world almost 200 years ago, but it certainly was. The cities of Paris, New York, and London were desperate for more furs. No supply could possibly fill the demand. There was good money to be made.

Because of the high stakes involved, battles were fought over trapping rights in the West. In addition to the severe dangers from natural enemies such as bad weather and wild animals, trappers jealously fought other trappers. Native Americans of one tribe would fight against another. Several major wars were even fought over the trapping rights in this part of the continent. Thousands of people lost their lives, all in the name of fashion. Everyone wanted the skin of the beaver.

This old drawing shows beaver on the banks of the Missouri River. *(Photo: Oregon Historical Society.)*

NOT THE FIRST

*T*he peak era of trapping in the Old West was from 1807 to 1843. That is when almost all of the American trappers operated in the area. Trapping and trading in the western part of the country had been going on for a long time, however, even though the nation itself was only a few decades old.

Native Americans, of course, had been hunting and trapping in the area since prehistoric times. There were white men, too, who had preceded the Americans.

The French were the first non-Indian trappers to visit the area. In the 17th and 18th centuries, French explorers and trappers came down from Canada. They were amazed at the number of

beavers in the lakes and streams of the West. They did much of their own trapping; however, they depended quite a bit on Indian trappers, too. Indians would visit a French trading post with armloads of pelts. The French traders would eagerly take the pelts, and in exchange offer the Indians pots and pans, beads, and colorful cloth—whatever the Indians found interesting.

The British were more than a little interested in owning a part of this wealth. The French and Indian Wars were fought between the British and the French, beginning in 1689. The wars were fought to decide who had the right to control the trading and trapping that went on in all of North America. The beaver trapping rights, specifically, were very important to both nations.

There were actually four French and Indian Wars. The final one ended in 1763. The British were at last victorious. After defeating the French for the final time, they started the Hudson Bay Company. This was a large, organized business that would hire trappers to bring the beaver pelts out of the wilderness. The pelts were then shipped back to England. Even after the American colonies won their independence from England, the Hudson Bay Company continued to operate in the western part of the continent.

A NEW RIVAL

North America in 1803—the western boundary of "Louisiana" wasn't known.

*I*n the year 1810 more and more American trappers and traders were making their way west. They were independent, which means that they did not work for a large company. They didn't receive regular wages, nor did anyone else provide them with supplies of food or ammunition, as was the case with trappers who worked for the Hudson Bay Company.

It was in this year that a German-born American named John Jacob Astor got involved in the business of beaver trapping. Astor was not a trapper himself; he was a businessman. His dream was to form a large trading company

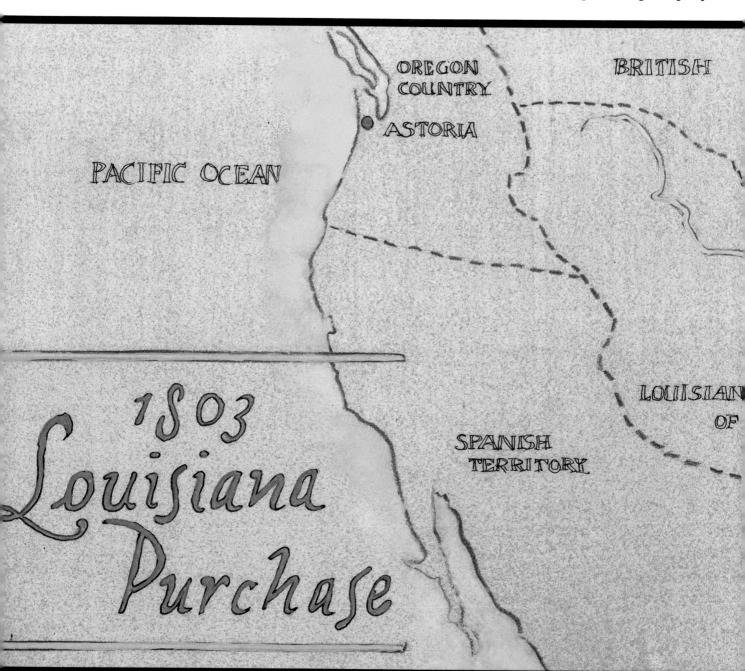

PACIFIC OCEAN

OREGON COUNTRY

ASTORIA

BRITISH

SPANISH TERRITORY

LOUISIAN
OF

1803 Louisiana Purchase

that would rival the British Hudson Bay Company in the far western part of the continent. (Remember that the areas that are now the states of Washington, Idaho, and Oregon, to name only a few, were not yet a part of the United States. They were simply areas that neighbored the Louisiana Territory. No one had a real claim to these areas. They hadn't been settled yet.)

Astor's plan seemed simple, at least on paper. He would send a large crew to Oregon Country, and would have them build a large trading post there. The spot Astor chose was on the mouth of the Columbia River. The trading post would be called Astoria (Astor had never been known for his modesty) and would be the largest post in the area. Trappers would come to Astoria from all over Oregon Country and sell their pelts.

The pelts would be loaded on ships and sent to China, a country that was eager to purchase furs from America. At the time, a firm from Boston was doing more than $500,000 a year in fur business with the Chinese. Astor's plan would be more practical from a business standpoint. Ships could leave directly from Astoria. At the time, ships had to sail from Boston, around Cape Horn at the tip of South America, then up to the Oregon coast.

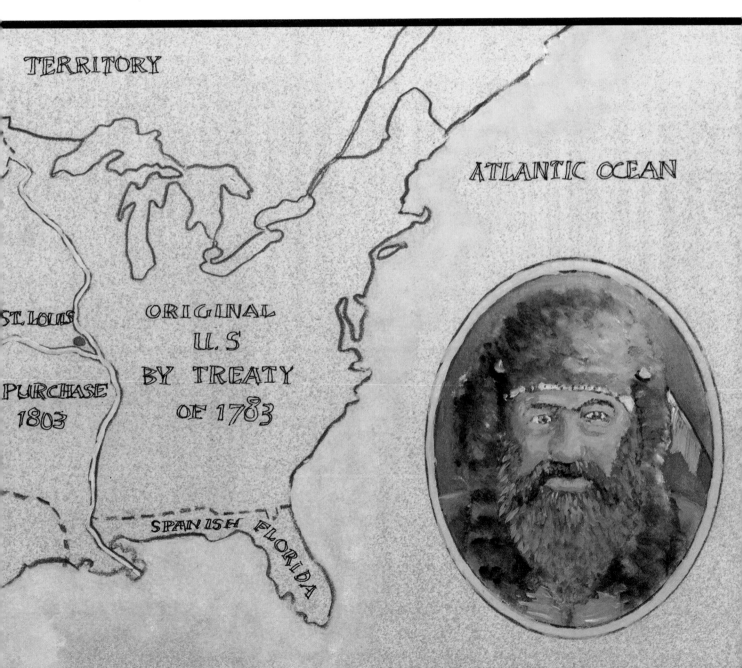

John Jacob Astor
(Photo: Denver Public Library. Western History Dept.)

THE SEAGOING ROUTE

*A*stor's plan succeeded only in giving the Americans a firmer foothold in Oregon Country. In most other respects, the venture failed.

He had planned that there would be two crews—one going by land, the other by sea around Cape Horn to the site of the new trading

post, Astoria. Both crews met with disaster.

The seagoing crew, traveling in an old ship called the Tonquin, was captained by a stern man named Jonathan Thorn. Thorn let out a smaller boat from the *Tonquin* when they reached the mouth of the Colombia River, although the seas were far too stormy and rough. The small boat went down, killing all on board.

Astor and a few of his advisors later got ashore and built the trading post, while the *Tonquin* roamed up and down the coast trading with Native American tribes. Captain Thorn stupidly insulted a chief during some of their dealings, and slapped the man across the face. This resulted in an Indian uprising that led to the deaths of the entire *Tonquin* crew.

Captain Thorn's action led to the deaths of the entire crew of the *Tonquin.*

THE OVERLAND ROUTE

*W*hat about the half of the crew that journeyed to Astoria by land? They intended to take the route that Lewis and Clark had used. However, they decided at the last minute to veer from the plan. They were concerned that the Blackfoot Indians might attack if the crew went over land, so they chose

to travel by canoe along the Snake River.

Several of the men were drowned when their dugout canoes were smashed against the canyons of the Snake River. Those who survived had to endure months of intense cold, blistering heat, and near-starvation. The survivors staggered into the little trading post of Astoria more than 18 months after leaving St. Louis!

And what became of Astoria? Unfortunately for Astor, the United States and England went to war in 1812. Eventually he had to surrender his trading post to the British—for a time, anyway. After the war, there were years of negotiations between the two nations, trying to settle the question of trapping and trading rights in Oregon Country.

Astor's overland crew met disaster in the canyons of the Snake River.

Although the British were firmly based in the area, the Americans had a bigger advantage. They were closer! Every day, more and more Americans were setting out for the West, eager to make their fortunes. Eventually, the British lost interest. They soon found it impractical to be thousands of miles from home, competing with a nation so near to Oregon Country. They left the West to the Americans.

TRAPPING IN THE OLD WEST

By 1820, trapping and trading was at its peak in the Old West. American fur companies, such as the newly formed Rocky Mountain Trading Company, had three different ways of obtaining the thousands and thousands of pelts they needed. The first was to trade with Indian trappers. The second was to hire trappers to travel into the wilderness, get pelts, and bring them back. The third was to deal with men who were in business for themselves, the independents. It is this third group, sometimes called "mountain men," that has captured the imagination of writers and storytellers through the years. These men were loners, people who enjoyed the solitude of the forests and mountains. They might have run into other trappers or a scouting party of Indians, but generally they preferred being by themselves. They were fiercely independent.

"THEY LOOKED LIKE INDIANS"

What was it like to be a mountain man in the the 1820's? In 1828 a newspaper writer from the East decided to interview some of the mountain men. He thought that it would be interesting for people to read about what the rugged, dangerous life was like.

When the writer was introduced to a few of the men, he was astonished. "It was amazing," he wrote. "These brave and hardy men would be mistaken for Indians by most folks. They are ruddy and dark of complexion, and their hair is matted and long. On more than one of the men, the locks were braided. They certainly look like Indians to me."

Indeed, many of the mountain men imitated the ways of the Indians they met. They learned, for example, that buckskin was a warm and cheap material for clothing. They soon wore loose-fitting buckskin shirts and pants. Experienced mountain men also knew that fringed buckskin was even better. The fringe

helped keep snow and rain off the shirts and pants themselves. (Moisture didn't really hurt the buckskin, but it made it hard and stiff.)

The mountain man wore moccasins, just as the Indians did. He spent much of his time wading in cold mountain streams as he set his traps, and moccasins were more durable and more practical than shoes and socks. In the winter, he would stuff his moccasins with dry grass for extra protection from the cold. The moccasins were made of buffalo hide, but not just any buffalo hide. The Indians taught the mountain men that it was important to use hide that had been seasoned, or treated with smoke. That kept the hide from shrinking when it became wet. A trapper who didn't know this secret would be in severe pain if he went to bed wearing wet, unseasoned moccasins. They could shrink and cut off the circulation in his feet!

Mountain men weren't completely uninterested in their appearance. A trapper's hat, for instance, was a source of pride. He looked at his hat as more than protection for his head. Many mountain men wore raccoon-skin hats, or leather hats decorated with beads and porcupine quills. One group of trappers that had originally come from Canada wore hats of bright blue. On each one dangled several wolves' tails. This was a statement of the trapper's bravery—it showed that he had experienced danger in the wilderness and had come away with a souvenir!

Trappers imitated many Indian ways.

"YOU AIN'T LIVED TILL YOU TASTED IT"

There were no mealtime schedules for a trapper. He ate when he was hungry, providing he had a supply of food. Sometimes he would go for days without seeing any game to kill. One mountain man told a story of being so hungry that he boiled his own moccasins and ate them!

When there was food to be found—and there usually was—the mainstay of the trapper's diet was meat. Almost 100 percent of his food came from animals or birds that he was able to shoot. Vegetables and fruits weren't available, except for wild berries. One mountain man told his grandchildren that he went for 17 years without tasting bread!

The favorite meat was buffalo—preferably a roast from the hump of the buffalo. Jim Bridger, probably the most famous of all mountain men, once said that a meal of buffalo meat is the nearest thing to being in heaven. "You ain't lived," he claimed, "till you tasted it."

The meat from a buffalo wasn't the only part that was edible. Trappers used the blood to make soup, and they cracked the bones to get iron-rich bone marrow. This marrow, called "trapper's butter," could be spread on dried meat, or used in soup. Raw buffalo liver was another choice part of the animal. Believe it or not, it was a favorite with mountain men.

Some of this food may sound strange or

Mountain men depended on their rifles—usually a "Hawken"—to get the meat they needed to survive. Because buffalo were plentiful and tasty, they were the most popular game to shoot.

unappetizing to you and me. But the mountain men thought they ate better than people who lived in civilization. In fact, the trappers' term for a rookie, or newcomer, was a French phrase—mangeur de lard, or "bacon eater." Trappers felt that if a man still had a taste for such "civilized" foods as bacon or ham, he had a long way to go before being called a mountain man!

RENDEZVOUS!

The word "rendezvous" is a French word, too. It means "a pre-arranged meeting or gathering." The annual rendezvous was the highlight for everyone who made a living selling pelts. It was the invention of a trader named William Ashley. The idea was simple—rather than have individual trading posts to which trappers brought their pelts, the traders would come to the trappers!

Beginning in 1822, traders from fur companies began to make the journey from St. Louis, and even farther east. They brought wagonload after wagonload of supplies for the mountain men and other trappers. The supplies could be "bought" with beaver pelts.

For the trapper who had been living far from any towns or stores for over a year, the rendezvous was extremely important. He could stock up on such luxuries as tobacco, gunpowder, new traps, sugar, coffee, and tea. More than a few mountain men were married to Indian women. If that was the case, the trapper would find beads, trinkets, blankets, mirrors, cooking pots, and other items that his wife would appreciate.

For all of these supplies, the currency was beaver pelts, or "plews," as the trappers called them. Some even jokingly nicknamed them "hairy bank notes!" A usual price for a pelt was $4, although during one rendezvous the going rate was $9. Some trappers brought in several hundred plews at one time. You might think they would walk away quite rich. You would be mistaken, however, because the traders—not the trappers—were in control of the deals.

The traders knew that the trappers needed supplies, and were, in many cases, quite desperate for them—especially gun powder. Traders kept their "prices" many times higher than the prices in a store in town. A blanket that sold in St. Louis for $5, for instance, might be purchased at the rendezvous for 15 plews—

worth $60-$135!

But the rendezvous was more than just business. It was a time to let off steam, to enjoy the company of other people. For many trappers, the rendezvous was the one time each year when they saw other humans!

There were feasts, parties, and dancing. The men spent long evenings around the campfires, listening to the exciting stories of other mountain men. They all liked to brag about how brave, how smart, and how clever they were. They really stretched their stories into tall tales!

There were also contests of every kind—horse racing, wrestling, shooting, and even drinking contests. It seemed as though the trappers tried to pack a year's worth of socializing into two short weeks. When the time was over, the trading wagons would head back east, and the trappers would go back into the mountains until the following year.

SOME OF THE MOUNTAIN MEN

There are many exciting stories about the trappers and traders of the Old West. The men and their adventures could fill 100 books. There was Jebediah Smith, who had the record number of beaver plews at a rendezvous—668! There was Jim Beckwourth, who was the son of a Southern farmer and a black slave. Because of his dark skin, he once convinced the angry Crow Indians that he was the long-lost son of their chief. His quick thinking saved his life, and he lived for six years as a member of the tribe. He was even made a chief!

As with any group of people, there are a few trappers of the Old West that have become quite famous. Their adventures have been told and retold around campfires for many generations. Two of these men stand out from the rest.

JIM BRIDGER

Probably the most famous of the mountain men was tall, muscular Jim Bridger. Nicknamed "Old Gabe" by his friends, Bridger was a man of many talents.

For one thing, he was an excellent shot. Other trappers reported seeing Jim ride his horse into the middle of a buffalo stampede and bring down 20 of the huge creatures with 20 shots!

Jim Bridger was a master at finding his way through the mountains.

Jim was also known for having a perfect memory—sometimes called a photographic memory. He could see something once, and it would be forever imprinted in his mind. That particular talent came in very handy when he was making his way through the dense forests of the Rocky Mountains. It also was valuable when he was traveling through country that was inhabited by different tribes of Indians. To stray into hostile territory—Blackfoot country, for instance—would be almost certain death for any trapper. Jim needed to see a path or trail only once, and he would never be lost again.

But probably the most interesting thing about Jim Bridger was his storytelling ability—mixed with his sense of humor. Jim was a master of the tall tale, and he could tell the most outrageous stories with a very straight face. He liked nothing more than to corner some young, inexperienced trappers and tell them one of his stories.

One of Jim's favorites was the story of trying to shoot a big moose. He took careful aim and fired, but the moose kept grazing on the green

grass. Jim said that he fired again and again, but the moose appeared not to notice. Convinced that he had shot accurately, he crept closer to the moose—and walked smack into a clear glass mountain! The moose was on the other side of the mountain, more than 15 miles away. Jim said he picked up his flattened bullets, got on his horse, and rode away.

The young trappers, listening in awe to Jim's stories, were astonished. They couldn't see the older trappers rolling their eyes and shaking their heads. It wasn't until Jim told his story of the eight-hour echo that the young men caught on.

There was a certain canyon, said Jim, that was so deep that a man could holler into it and the sound wouldn't come back for eight hours. It was particularly useful for waking up in the morning. All you had to do, explained Jim with a serious expression on his face, was yell "Time to get up!" just before you went to bed at night. The next morning you'd be awakened by your own voice, coming back to you!

Jim Bridger
(Photo: Oregon Historical Society.)

JOHN COLTER'S RACE FOR LIFE

Another famous trapper was John Colter, who had been part of the Lewis and Clark expedition. He loved the new country so much that he decided to stay. Colter had been trapping with a partner, a man named Potts. They found themselves in an area inhabited by the hostile Blackfoot Indians. When the two men were confronted by a party of Blackfeet, Potts panicked, picked up his rifle, and shot one of the Indians. At a signal from their chief, the other warriors shot Potts with a volley of arrows.

The Blackfoot chief ordered that Colter, too,

should die. The chief decided that the Indians would shoot Colter down like a hunted animal. Colter was ordered to strip off all of his clothes, including his moccasins. On a signal from the chief, Colter was to run, chased by the war party of Blackfeet. He had a 300-yard head start.

Did Colter run! He paid no attention to the stones and the sharp prickly bushes. He ran on bruised and bleeding feet, with the Blackfeet right on his heels, and didn't stop until he came to the Madison River six miles away.

When he came to the river, he dove in and swam under a beaver dam. The sticks and mud

John Colter's race for life was to last for seven days and cover 200 miles!

kept him hidden from view until the Indians finally gave up looking. He stayed there all night, and then set out again. He continued his frightening race for seven more days. Every so often, he'd look nervously over his shoulder, not sure if more Blackfeet had picked up his trail. Still naked and badly bruised, he reached Fort Manuel, some 200 miles from where he had started!

CHANGING TIMES

hese were exciting times, but they didn't last very long. By the late 1830's the days of the trappers and traders had just about come to an end. One reason for this was that there were fewer and fewer beavers to be trapped. Once the lakes and streams had been filled with the animals, but the years of heavy trapping had thinned their numbers considerably.

The other reason for the end of the trapping and trading was changing fashions. Beaver felt simply wasn't in demand. Plews that once sold for $4 were worth less than $1 in 1836. People

in the cities no longer wore beaver hats. They were now buying hats made of silk from China.

It seems strange that so much energy was spent on the beaver trade when it was based on something as changeable as fashion. Wars were fought, and thousands of people died. Relations between white Americans and Native Americans became angry and violent at times.

But for all the negative things that happened, the exploits of the trappers and mountain men of the Old West were valuable, too. These men were true pioneers—they were the first settlers to open the Louisiana Territory and Oregon Country. In the years that followed, more settlers came to the areas that were once uncharted wilderness. The paths they followed had been mapped out by the fur traders and trappers. The stories of these trappers and traders, combined with their legends and tall tales, are truly an important part of the history of the American West.

For 40 colorful years, the mountain men contributed to the history of the American West.

TRAVELING LIGHT

*T*he trapper didn't have a lot of possessions. He knew that everything he owned he had to carry around with him, so he was careful about the things he kept!

Every trapper used a mule. The animal was not ridden—it was used as a luggage carrier. The mule was led on a rope made of horsehair. On its back were all the heavy tools of the trapper's trade—and other necessities, as well. The mule carried sleeping blankets, beaver pelts, and perhaps the carcass of a deer or other animal the trapper had shot for food.

In addition, the mule carried the traps needed to catch the beavers. Each trapper used about six steel traps, which he guarded with his life. Traps were expensive—usually about $15 each, which was a lot of money in those days. Some dishonest trappers stole other men's traps. Sometimes, too, a trap was lost because it was set incorrectly and the beaver pulled it free.

Also strapped to the mule's back were several smaller sacks. One contained dried beef, called jerky, and nuts or fruit. Another sack, made of buckskin or buffalo skin, had little odds and ends that could possibly prove useful in the wilderness. For that reason, mountain men called this their "possible sack." Sometimes a possible sack contained a small scissors, a supply of tobacco, and a pipe. Other times, the trapper would carry in his possible sack extra deerskin for mending torn moccasins, a lucky coin, or an interesting rock he picked up along the way.

The mule was useful in another way, besides carrying the trapper's supplies. For some unknown reason, mules were excellent guards. Their powerful sense of smell enabled them to know when a stranger

was nearby. If an Indian or another trapper dared to come too near to the campsite, the mule would bray a loud alarm. This warning sometimes saved a trapper's life!

Even though he depended on his mule, the trapper had to carry his share of the load, too. Every trapper carried a blackpowder rifle—most often a Hawken, made by St. Louis gunsmith Jake Hawken. The Hawken rifle was shorter than the Kentucky rifle, and because it used a copper cap, it was better in rainy weather. Trappers boasted that they could kill a grizzly bear or a buffalo 200 yards away with their Hawken rifles.

The trapper carried a supply of balls (round lead bullets) in a pouch hung over his shoulder. He also carried a cow's horn filled with gunpowder, and small greased "patches." The patches were needed to hold the balls on top of the gunpowder.

Every trapper needed a knife, both for protection and for skinning the animals he trapped. The knife was kept in a sheath attached to his belt. The trapper would wipe his knife on his buckskin pants or shirt to add to the grease on them already. Although this wiping made the clothing smelly and stained, it also made the material even more waterproof!

The final bit of equipment worn by the trapper was an antelope horn filled with what he called "medicine." What it actually contained was castoreum, a strong-smelling liquid taken from behind the tail of a dead beaver. Castoreum is used by beavers to mark out their territories (for food or mating) in a river.

The trapper took advantage of this knowledge by using the smelly liquid to lure beavers to the traps. The trapper would wade through the icy water of a mountain river, so as not to leave any human smell. He then would set the trap, rubbing castoreum on a nearby clump of grass with a willow twig. When a beaver would come to investigate the familiar smell, he would be caught in the jaws of the trap.

Everything needed to survive in the mountains had to be carried by either the trapper or his mule.

IN THE DAYS OF THE TRAPPERS AND TRADERS

1535	Jacques Cartier, a Frenchman, sails his ship up the St. Lawrence River. He is the first white explorer to travel inland in North America. He brings furs back to France.
1620	The *Mayflower* sets sail from England to America.
1670	England's Hudson Bay Company founded.
1763	The last of the French and Indian Wars is over. France loses all her land and trade holdings in the New World to Britain.
1770	Population of the United States is 2,205,000.
1775	A woman is appointed postmaster in Baltimore.
1776	America wins independence from England.
1777	Vermont becomes the first place in the United States to abolish slavery.
1787	The U.S. Constitution signed.
1795	The first circus performs in the United States. It was called Rickett's Circus, from England.
1808	John Colter races 200 miles to escape a Blackfoot Indian tribe.
1810	John Jacob Astor founds Pacific Fur Company.
1812	England and America are at war.
1813	John Colter dies in St. Louis.
1820	Daniel Boone dies at age 85.
1835	Hans Christian Andersen writes his first fairy tale.
1836	Arkansas becomes the 25th state.
1837	Martin Van Buren sworn in as eighth President of the United States.
1839	Congress outlaws dueling in the District of Columbia.
1839	The rules of the game of baseball are first written down.
1843	End of beaver trade in the West.
1859	Charles Blondin walks on a tightrope across Niagara Falls.
1866	The nickel coin is authorized by Congress.
1881	Former mountain man Jim Bridger dies.